Only You Can Say

Only You Can Say: New and Selected Poems

Guy Craig

Oregon, USA

ONLY YOU CAN SAY:
NEW AND SELECTED POEMS

Published by
www.GuyCraigPoetry.com
ISBN: 978-1-7334968-7-2

© Copyright 2025 by GUY CRAIG
Portland, Oregon

Written by Guy Craig
Artwork and Cover Design by SARAH CRAIG

For inquiries, write to the author, with the subject line "Inquires," at the email address below:

GuyCraigPoetry@gmail.com

Visit - www.GuyCraigPoetry.com

Many of the poems in the volume were previously published in *Coos River Reverberations: Poems of River, Farm & Forest* (2021); *Amble: Poems* (2021); *Idling Intuitions: Poems* (2022); *Mast Years: Poems* (2022).

*For Sarah,
Kenneth & Stella*

CONTENTS

Only You Can Say: New Poems

4	Only You Can Say
5	Little Blue Door
6	Today, You're 44
7	Trail Between Dreams
8	In the Wilderness
9	Career Reprieve
10	Recipes From Coos River
12	Diminishing Returns
13	Eyes Closed, I Dream
14	How Long We Wait . . .
15	Echoes From My Younger Days
16	A Safe Someday
17	Two Worlds
19	Mixed Feelings
20	The News: An Elegy
22	Observations
23	Continuous Improvement
24	Recreate or Retire
25	Your Other Gifts

CONTENTS

26	Until It's Gone
27	Body of Water
28	Moss-Threaded Possibilities
29	Six Months
30	Erode the Sky
31	On Your Side
32	The Distance Between
34	Last Breaths
35	Shadows From Your Setting Sun
36	Absence
37	Better Tomorrow
38	River Freshet
39	Walking Away
41	Seekers of Power
42	Compulsion and Choice
44	Shapes of Shadows
45	Turning the Gravel
46	Against the Current
47	Wrapped Wilderness
48	Silt and Mud
49	Swell
50	Below the Surface
51	Abundance
52	I Cast the Sand
53	Two Birds
54	Remaining Light
55	On the River We Float II

CONTENTS

Coos River Reverberations: Poems of River, Farm & Forest

58	Tidal River Swimming Hole
59	Mr. Buzzard
61	Night Swimming
63	Stars
64	Looking Out the Classroom Window
66	Afternoon Music Hour
68	A Summer Home
70	A Riverside Garden Work Party
72	Homemade Smoker
74	Salmon on the Fire Pit
75	Gone Too Soon
77	Barbed Wire
79	Outworked
81	The Windstorm
83	Blue Smoke Around the Card Table
85	Cow Jam
89	Himalayan Blackberry
91	Woodstove in the Old Ranch House
92	To Town
94	A Walk up the Draw to Recharge
96	When I Grow Up
100	Chittum Bark
102	Maple Leaves Piled in the Dry Creek Bed
104	Myrtle Grove
107	Living Near the Stream
109	Froze Last Night
111	Dusk

CONTENTS

Amble: Poems

113	Amble
114	When We Help
115	Measure of Loss
116	Fox Gloves
117	Broadleaf Dock
118	Infused Path
119	Potted Oregon Myrtle
120	On the Mountain
121	Moss Over Wood Ash
122	Summer Reflection
123	Bouquet of Nettles
124	I Long for the Rain
125	Oregon Myrtle Trees
126	A Stop at the Dock

Idling Intuitions: **Poems**

128	Travel Without Touring
129	Arrived
131	Patience
132	Tolerance
133	Ways Once Lived

CONTENTS

Mast Years: Poems

135   Stories of Home
136   Other Worlds Have I
138   Flower Arrangements
139   Cutting Boards
140   Retired Neighbors

142   Afterword

Only You Can Say: Poems

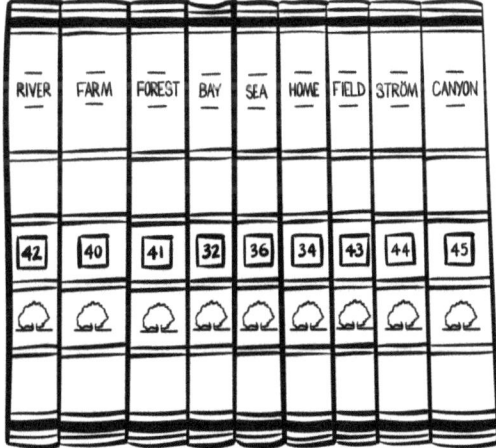

New Poems

Only You Can Say (2025)

Only You Can Say

Only You Can Say

You said the word "no" for the first time today.
You turned down one more sip of milk. A sentiment
you shared without words before in so many wordless ways—
sharp cries, fluttering lip sighs, and flailing movements of dismay.

I looked at your mother when you told her.
We both celebrated your voice, and I know
we both hid our mixed feelings through our happy displays.
Commencements are like that—one journey has ended,

another awaits, and those who have loved you the longest
will miss what you may not remember.
Today, you said the word "no" for the first time.
A new word we hope to teach you

how to ignore and how to obey.
Though it may take endless tomorrows,
we will listen to what you say next.
Will it be "yes?" Only you can say.

Little Blue Door

There you go again out the front door.
The one you once called your own.
The little blue door on a little winding road
that welcomed you home. Until this morning,

when you closed it and dared to become
someone rare, someone fare, someone who cares
where life might lead. We saved all these years
to give you a chance to learn, to grow, to become

a little more of who you are—more developed,
knowledgeable, and refined. We saved all these years
to give ourselves a chance to learn, to grow, to become
more of what you might need of us when you are less

developed than you deserve, less prepared for the pain
you will suffer in this world, and when you reach your goals
for exploration and find your version of a little blue door
on a little winding road and realize why,

with all the wonders and welcomes you've known,
even in joy, you sometimes cry. Life doesn't stay dry.
The terrarium of your truth isn't broken. There's just little light.
The views you'll remember best are between day and night.

Today, You're 44

Today, you're 44. The Julys before
are cake. All the aromatic jasmine
flowers belaying on the nearby trees
are woven hammocks with river views.

Softness near the sand and time
flow in all directions to this moment.
Almost an echo—a relative of a rhyme.
All wishes are welcome. One will arrive

and you'll answer: "Here I am. Here I'll stay.
What do I wish for? Only—others find peace
where sand greets the water and the summer
evening winds dance with willows and sing of play."

Trail Between Dreams

I listen for the hum of quiet
spring and summer gatherings in a private field
of fragrant flowers full of family and close friends
with perennially pleasing flower arrangement hopes.

Maybe I was born 100 years too late.
I live in a small world that is almost too large.
I have two sights: I see the stream of traffic
out the living room window of my new city,

and I remember western redcedar bows holding the damp dew
of the morning with my rural, childhood, canyon home
full of beautiful art legacies and the kindling of woodstove moments
for family comfort. I hold dearly to the eternal tomes and talismans

of spring and summer smiles from hillside gardens.
Will an old kind of awareness find me?
I'll follow myrtle spices in the air and get caught
by a fixed-weight, summer-hammock-woven-memories leader

of soft, hook scents from alder
campfire wood smoke fragrances that frame
my old and new scenes as I teach
my children—*life is more than a trail between dreams.*

In the Wilderness

In the wilderness, loneliness is overcome by the guide runners
of our connections to family and friends. A good sense
of direction can replace city signs. This morning, everything

is listening to the whispers of willows. The weather is calm,
the air tastes like sea salt, and my skin runs with the oil
of myrtle leaves. All paths are thinking about summer grass.

Gray, dusty gravel roads and iron-infused stones in creeks cross
winding canyon floral greens to home. Open doors have music
inside meandering around corners, collections, and crosses.

Rhododendron dreams and huckleberry hopes unhook from holes,
rocks behind mosses, and new bark over old winter storm scars.
Full pitchers of iced tea and half-drunken bottles of hard cider

cast late afternoon, amber streams of light through the hinges
of our family reunion and potluck memories. Fall out
of an inner tube on an incoming tide, knock over a split-rail fence

in a game of catch, and carry all the grass and sand—wet,
bare feet can hold—along the distance from just right of the old
apple tree and slightly beyond the year's suffering and loss.

Career Reprieve

How much more work is needed
to finally earn the free time you seek
for a well-timed career reprieve?

Does anyone know where to draw the line
to mark the midway of life's decline?
At the movies, intermissions have become novel.

You might find them in silent films which still reflect
answers in the dim, black-and-white shades between lines.
What is a year or two

away from the saturated lights of professional praise,
when you get to trade monetary ease for more time
with the family of your dreams whom you love to please?

Recipes from Coos River

Recipes from Coos River: Summer on the South Fork
is the title we chose for your cookbook.
A mouthful? Recipes are a funny thing.
They allow a level of precision into a home

where opacity often reins. We can't separate our tears
underwater in our wakes. Recipes teach us ways
to fill myrtle bowls with more than the bounty
from cold, winter soil amendments and spring rains.

The cookbook author is away.
My need for precision remains. The recipes are before me.
All I want to do is forget—this day, this tray.
Not your laugh, the way you arch your right ear to hear,

nor your often wild-eyed attention to details
deemed time-sensitive or your harried sounds
in the face of duties deemed unending.
Cooking on the fire pit rack takes focus,

especially if a host's helper is pretending.
I don't see you at the end of the dinner table.
You would buy the freshest ingredients, prep, cook,
and clean. Now our table is unstable. What happened

in between? The fishing line changed its angle?
The net flowed with the tides and it was let go?
I saw the river current of your life run up a creek
and follow the farewell call of a hummingbird.

I've seen enough for one day. I think
I'll make a myrtle-infused gin and tonic.
It's a simple recipe. I'll get it wrong.
You'd say—*mistakes are a matter of taste.*

Diminishing Returns

I am not ready for life's diminishing returns.
My trips home are still restorative. Retiring
from something instead of to something is something
I fear.

I want continuous joy from the countless connections
I have held together over the years with my family and friends.
I don't want family and friends to be less necessary
or loved at a distance. I want us to continue to want to return

to a place we all praise. On each trip home,
I will give a toast for good health and good fortune
that our traditions perdure with each generation near soft songs
of the ocean and with strong trees holding hands as deep roots.

Eyes Closed, I Dream

City crowds can move as smoothly as threads through silk.
Buildings rise to heights even light dares to tread. Ask the dead.
For some, everything in the countryside is replaceable.
Who needs iron-infused creeks where stoplights shine red?

I once cared about diffused summer light, under myrtle trees,
away from the city. I'd measure the degrees of dampness
from the river water in my hair on my ambles from my family's
sandbar through the fields to the garden gate that was always open.

Deer and rabbits can't hurt a fence laid down to be fixed. The afternoon
of my life is far from the glow of moonlight off the edges of leaves
in their sleep caught between the stars and the breeze, hidden bees,
careful caterpillars, and songs between trees. Eyes closed, I dream.

How Long We Wait . . .

—silhouettes of people
with words on the edges
of a fading picture.

—rocks, convex shaped—
skipping on smooth water.

—when a chrysalis becomes
a caterpillar.

—when a seed becomes
a sprout.

matters.

Echoes From My Younger Days

When you live near a coastal river,
sound often carries off river rock walls in the wind.
I often hear the faint echoes of my younger days.

Did I hear a call? My joy was the likely source.
I listen. The sunset warms my gray hair. I tell my children
to keep playing loudly and to laugh until they're hoarse.

A Safe Someday

As a child, all the neighbors lived near
the myrtle-veiled road that led
to a little chapel on a hill
overlooking the river valley fields below,

drained by old hands with new shovels held close
by their young children. Shadows passed over them
like the memories they left to be buried on other shores.
I am in awe of their trust and belief in family and friends

to find a place to grow a more enduring, nurturing nature.
I give thanks for my time within that nascent, rural
freedom where my ancestor's dreams of a safe someday,
cherished by all in the sweetness of the last days of summer,

was briefly and appreciatively achieved. I was formed
from one land. A new person foretold in loud cries of loss mixed
with old echoes of steady, stored tears for a happier tomorrow.
By generations from an old land, I was raised to question

and avoid others' unrelenting claims
and anonymous answers. I was taught to resist
urgent calls for utopias forced on us through pain.
I'm still learning

how to securely sew together siren songs of leisure
with finely woven threads of truth discovered
in the drained lands of a tidal river valley by those seeking
the grace of healing and the fading of echoes from past hurts.

Two Worlds

In my mind, only two worlds exist: Portland and Coos Bay.
The left and right hemispheres of my brain hold them
together. In me—the outrunning of a tsunami while I drive
along a river road with many places where the levees wane.

How can I not question what passes near and away
from me? Blink and a brisk bridging of all the tapestries
of reasons for my time away are woven together, one by one,
like summer hammocks between trees moving in the breeze

in the rhythmic strum of my memories while light scatters through
strong branches and the magnetic array of iron-infused leaves.
I wince at the misplaced confidence of my youth. Can I understand
and unravel what is eternal in both from what time measures in me?

Mixed Feelings

When I fall, I fall early and late. I try to keep the time.
After a loss, life has a way of making
the middle path clear in review.
It is hard to know

the best decisions to make for future generations.
Those born away from the influence of the land
may no longer be able to relate to the peculiar,
aching attachments land requires one to maintain.

Who will they become in their own time without the land?
What type of experiences in the world will wrap
their consciousness? Will they hold our history as dear?
My time connected to the family lands I own

may be over. The decision wasn't made in haste.
Is this the right time to be replaced?
Choosing the land was made early and late.
I write now so my mixed feelings will not be erased.

The News: An Elegy

Have you heard? All the news
is broken. All the new colors are burnt
shades of yellow from newspapers in disarray.
Anything made or powered by the politics of politeness

can break, die, rot, and fade
away. Even grizzled journalists have stopped
questioning if people can smile with every excuse.
I traced a string of code to the merger of America

Online with Time Warner on January 10th, 2000.
That year, natural rights (unofficially) became untenable
at the United Nations. Have you ever had unguarded
conversations and let lovers of gaslighting attend?

Was it not Socrates, but Athenian jurors who were ugly?
Did M. J. Adler improve Aristotle and St. Augustine too bluntly?
A.I. sees your query. . . A.I. may hallucinate if you hurry . . .
the long progression of questioning perennial problems and

similarities of families, groups, tribes, villages, towns, cities, states,
and countries as one world and one government became one
big recusal. Was it excusable? With money, power is useful.
The U.N. couldn't measure Western truth, but Eastern harmony

felt less rough. Only fine sand gets washed through the cracked
glass of a decorative hourglass. Some researchers believe
a fast-burning flame of words was spun in people's eyes
to enhance inattention. 111 articles say that both East and West

love ascension. Current research says undogmatic ideas are in old,
buried, retention walls of dry wells left to sit. Great online libraries
are the harvested waters to drink and quench thirst as a store of
unreplicable research for free, and behind paywalls, free speech

for all for a small fee. Society's time has not been wasted curating performative, broken, dead, rotted links. I am harmonious and sweet. The truth is broken. A stat was hacked. This job has Ivy League prestige. It's beyond history. Truth hides with recluses and the muses.

All the definitions have confusing negative connotations anyway. Let's play! Let's plant a probability. Influenza of what we say? You live. Sad song? Some pray to silicon as the savior of the day. Bow? Bend? It's okay. Faded-yellow-journalistic-algorithms still report—sell in May.

Observations

I found a way to reveal all the ideas I set aside
for better days and thoughtful times.

I found a way to reveal all the feelings I set aside
from my younger days before I saw I was destined to decline.

I found a way to reveal all the world's lessons I set aside
from the discounted dreams I left untried.

I found a way to reveal how many of my life's obligations
were merely my insecurities in disguise. Why let others decide?

Continuous Improvement

For most of my life, I cared
About continuous improvement.
High expectations eclipsed
All other considerations. Little else mattered.
When you read Plato at eight
You get some high ideals. Great
Books came in a set of 54.
The best of the West was
All that ever attracted my attention.
I was Rodin's *The Thinker*
With a Coos Bay mullet,
A converted garage with four walls
Of dusty and torn books to read,
And a silly child to a second grandfather
Who cared about education and training
Someone to be admired. He passed
The torch of knowledge too early
Through chainsaw-smoke advice
For my liking and his comfort.
At 79 there is still life to grow and refine.
He was diligently trying to prepare
A serious politician or even a partial philosopher,
But I was a reclusive poet. Quick
To tears (like him) when reading
Longfellow's, *My Lost Youth*.
Older now, I've let go of high ideals.
When I read the poem, *The Day is Done*,
I pray I've written some fair poems
As a local history of family feelings
Worthy of a grandfather who would understand
A politician, a philosopher, or a poet
Are all chasing the gifts of the theologians
Who work tirelessly, if imperfectly,
For the world to share in the sweet
"Benediction that follows after prayer."

Recreate or Retire

Two homes in heart and mind is a life divided:
work or retire? When I win all my probable dreams
maybe I will understand my desire.
I take a step toward my future.

I fill my hopes with late morning and early evening
spring memories. Emerald green leaves and surprising spring
snow flows with my dreams on old-growth, logjam freshets
that float past the open gates of my childhood home.

Your Other Gifts

If you're lucky enough, you might
Begin to appreciate all the gifts
You've developed. For some, that's confirmation
Of a meaningful life. The foundation
Of your gifts—sown as seeds.
Every new skill is a blossom.
All paths are pressed and cleared of tangled roots
And unraveled for you to follow home. Someday,
Your gifts might illuminate the path for others
As you pass near the answers you've always known,
While the sweet breeze, now full of recognition,
Whispers, "Fallen petal, stem and reed—
You are a brief moment—
In this temperate rainforest, so be still. Follow me
On this rich earth, in the swirling sky above,
And within and below the waters of the humble sea."

Until It's Gone

I'm probably going to lose it up here.
If I go quiet, you *know* . . .
Oh, and don't we know
the way it goes.

The way it has been.
The way it will be.
We, here, more together today.
We, here . . . more thoughtful tomorrow.

A little closer to questions to endure.
A little closer to answers to obscure.
A love, a light, a life, we long—
a little more time—until it's gone.

Body of Water

I saw the glare of the sun in a body of water.
It was the evening color of forest smoke in September.
It was the sheen of dusty soil on debarked sticks.
Holding my hands over a passing reflection, all I could see

were potholes, ruts, and hollow roots cut and scratched
where once only yellow and purple iris memories were stored.
Shaded, burnt trees and gray grass marked off black
buzzards of different sizes. I turned my back

in disgust and dragged myself out of the dark
well of my discontent. Then, I slid back in—
through the silver foliage of fate—still old,
yet steady. I let my fear pour out. I was ready.

Moss-Threaded Possibilities

Stories settle into the evergreen
leaves with moss-threaded possibilities.
They layer below the November

dampness of a collapsing gravestone.
Brackish waters set the scene:
eight pallbearers shatter raindrops

across the moon. The mouth of a tugboat
splinters three times. Through a mist of tears,
a child cries, "port," from the bow.

Six Months

Up to six months they say. The paperwork can be renewed,
not you—just the paperwork. Some things are settled.
Rolling river fields must return to coastal mountain ranges.
Forest foliage turns ditches into dark wells.

Straight fence lines get bent into circles.
Fence posts get painted black. Winter water runoff
and shadows are a mixed drink for a view of the edge
of moving light. You stare blankly at the faces

you don't know. Those who love you, remember.
Lack of words cut and split wide open our darkest regrets.
You will face the cold. Only, *our* cheeks will turn red.
You won't be alone. Together, we all leave pain unsaid.

Erode the Sky

I infuse dreams in the land.
They become real when they leave my lungs.
The air becomes more like me.
I become more like dust.

I take a shortcut to a rag and bucket
where I am washed and dried.
I evaporate and scatter in the darkness
and erode the sky.

On Your Side

The rain takes a contrary bend through the sawdust,
spur spikes, and the dark engine smoke in my mind.
It mixes with my tears. It curls and turns this day
upside down in the winding river shallows of your outgoing tide.
All I hear below me is an estate of sounds I don't want

from the discrete parcels of your chest. Salt-worn metal skids
through gravel on the edge of its sharpness. A sheet falls off
your shoulders like split sandstone off a sterile shovel—the fabric lies
about how long you will need it as you lay on your side
and face away. Blackout curtains conceal an old forest

of gray, hollow stumps with roots that have gone cold.
Memories of your smile lay crosswise in the middle of my grief.
You stare at a painting of curves in a creek. I imagine you
along a calm riverbank. Hospice says it's time to tell you to
let go. *You can let go.* I know you *can't* be replaced.

The Distance Between

You flat-lined three times on your way to the hospital.
The EMT asked if you saw a light,
spoke with a family member, or heard a song.
"There was nothing," you said.

"Everything is darkness.
It isn't happy or sad, but it's still a bit disconcerting
for an old believer in an afterlife"
(which you told us later you no longer were).

You said there wasn't a distance between
the two worlds you could see, or taste, or feel in any way
that upon awakening might have made shitting
yourself at the hospital any less

embarrassing for you.
They say that happens
when you come back from death.
You clear your bowels.

Maybe your death was a message
to live better, to love more,
to understand that that is how life is sometimes—bad
sounds and smells arrive

along with a second chance.
Or, maybe it was nothing—*nowhere,*
where you don't need to ask for forgiveness
from those you've hurt or need to forgive

so you can heal, or see, or speak, or hear
in the distance between awareness and absolution.
Somewhere, you lived four lives and survived three deaths.
At the end, a falling leaf can float on other leaves' breaths.

Last Breaths

Sleep is a fawn's silhouette
in the shadows of darkness.
Fresh bedding, cool but not chill,
is a shortcut to the unseen.

Your last breaths are a layer of fog on a hill's
ragged edge with flickering views
of a family cemetery overlooking a tidal river
maintained with shovels, hoes, and rakes.

Shadows From Your Setting Sun

You are the soft breeze in an empty room I pass by.
You are the uncounted flower arrangements I planned
and failed to make in your honor. That day,
salutations lost all their significance.

Silence echoes its way to everywhere I can't listen.
You must have followed the tide to the barriers of solitude.
The delirious tide kept observantly in rhythm.
You are the ash as valediction in the water

the ground will let flow. All you were, all you loved,
is next to you in the shadows from your setting sun.
The memories of your health are hard to count.
They say the final days are like that.

In our wealth at home, you have become flowers arranged
by others in new vessels of consolation as your old, tended
flower beds outside lie down with fallen petals in red and yellow
light. I can tilt the sand of an hourglass, I *can't* turn back time.

Absence

The indent at the end of the couch looks lower today.
It shouldn't. No one has sat there.
Maybe it's how the light shines through the window
casting a shadow. While you were here,

the indent was a daily reminder that we needed a new couch.
"Wear it out" was our motto. It served us well—
until it wore out. Now, *I'm* worn out.
I'm left wondering—what comes next?

I ordered a new couch today—the one you wanted.
It won't have your indent—just an absence.
The light may not cast the same shadow.
It won't need to—*you* will always be with me.

Better Tomorrow

I saw you at the beach today.
You could be me. Were you delaying?
Are your dreams also *graying*? Through the fog,
I saw you cast the grains of tilled mountains.

You let them slip through your open and elevated fingers
with a resolve that life is what it could be.
Your hands followed your fingers to a smoothed,
colorless Oregon sunstone. You smiled

and you laughed, though I could barely hear it, below
the hymn of the wind in bent branches, pinned tree limbs,
and the crash of jetty-smashed waves. I let the tsunami
of sounds sail over my shoulders and bury my tears

where the low tide runs a line between sand and the years.
I cupped my hands like a broken bowl over my face and let
yesterday come to an end. Will there be a better tomorrow?
The fog may roam—sunlight shone where sunstones were sown.

River Freshet

How do you tell someone you're too far gone?
How do you explain that all that remains—
after last year's river freshet—is your regret?
It's a sharp shot of salt-packed clay

chased with an oily, iron future.
You have become the smell of minus tide,
the scent of two feet of river soil
wrapped around withering willow seeds of loss.

You have a volunteer crop you don't want.
It will bring years of lost pay. You search for new ways
through the pain of drowned promises. How do you
get back to some semblance of who you were?

Maybe you'll find yourself
again in time—just a bit more time.
You pull on cracked boots. Sink less in the silt.
You follow your muddy toes.

Walking Away

"Don't fall in love with the land," he told my father,
one week before he sold off the last parcel he owned.
The one with a lovely home overlooking the river,
where his mother and father passed away

peacefully together within days of each other.
The lovely home where he raised four children.
The lovely home with his family's dairy
and lower and upper fields rich with creeks,

ponds, forests, river banks,
and memories.
His children and others found each barn
as an adventure. All the paths on the property

were bad for bikes
and appropriate for taking chances.
Feeding calves bottles, scooping grain,
and throwing hay bails

was a lifestyle
and a gift for all the families with children
who didn't farm anymore.
All the nearby farms were leased to him.

Everyone else had jobs in town,
vacations far away, and fewer memories filled
with the fatigue of two daily milkings
and no weekends off.

He remembered. He felt whole when he fell in love with the land. He left that feeling of creation for the new owners in each piece of land he slowly let go.

Seekers of Power

Under the weight of a shoe,
old ash is underfoot.
It is coal black and exhausted.
In the distance, direct flames

on the edges ignite a dragging rope.
With a pack of cigarettes worth of energy,
tear ducts run dry and cryptic definitions
are applied to well-known words.

Old ideas are burned. Seekers of power
shift and dance in the low-hanging smog.
They say justice is what you make it.
Imagination hides in knotholes, slots, and cracks.

Compulsion and Choice

Compulsion and *Choice* fought in the high winds.
Their blood in the mist became the chill-morning
that sharpens its teeth on routine.
It stands next to a logger on a coastal mountain.

With a river-eye for profit, it calculates
how many loads of logs, lumber, and woodchips
can be shipped to Asia. A logger falls a tree.
His heart is away thinking about a girl

who will leave him. In his slumbered mind,
he checks off the day's activities. Bad fortune
falls and smoothers his final dreams to its chest.
He becomes fallen branches.

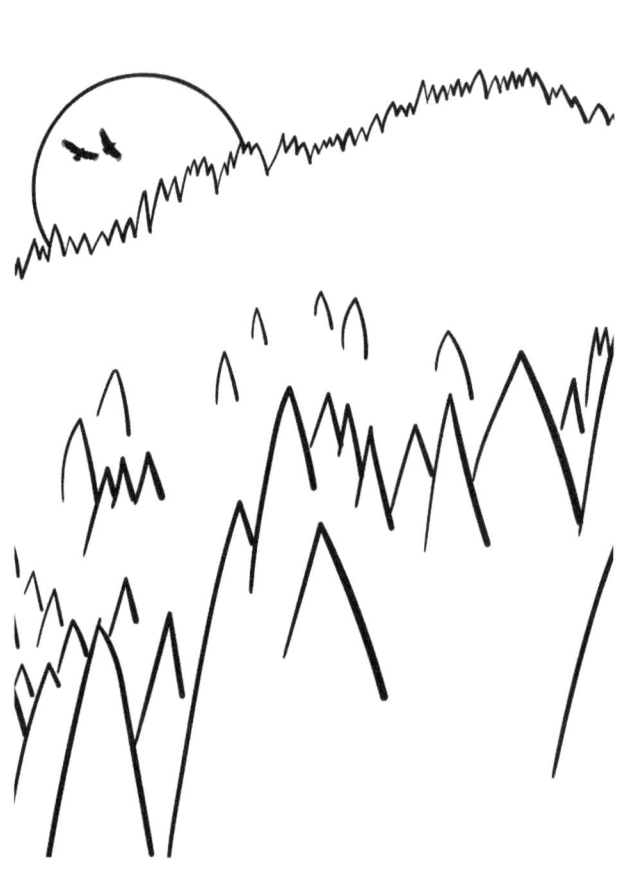

Shapes of Shadows

My memories are shapes of shadows
running along the bay. They cut below
shallows before a sandbar. I see shreds
of green fishing net, lost pots, rings off of rock

walls, and the glimmer of distant dune graveyards
full of faded beer cans and rusted tailpipes.
Rot in peace. Each summer, I regenerate a new shell.
I look ready to catch. I'm hollow between the meat

and the shell. Find me in September at the entrance
to the ocean. I turn into scars. I don't care
if life only gives me bottom fins to eat, I'll survive.
I figure out the tides, then set them to the side with relief.

Turning the Gravel

You drove down the driveway,
the tires turning the gravel.
Your heart is scraps of lumber,
splitting mauls, and chicken wire.

You are raw skin with claws on the pelt.
You're alive. You're a sun in a circle.
You run a slug circuit under the shade
of sticker bushes. You scratch the ground

with your boots. You knock the fates
with the hot coffee in your thermos.
You know where bears hide as skeletons.
You're not crab bait.

Against the Current

The wind picked up out of nowhere.
He smelled the incoming tide.
His stomach turned with the bay.
The fishing reel at his chest ran fast

and became his beating heart. He was tired of trolling
against the current of last chances. He caught the line
of his memories with both hands. He knew where to go.
He cranked hard on the engine throttle, and he watched

the last of its black smoke billowing in the air behind him.
His future stood next to an amber-colored creek.
He dodged deadheads below the surface. With his hands,
he moved past mud-spackled tree limbs of past blooms.

He found an old cow trail cut in the willows.
His hands became fishing nets for his hopes.
He climbed the old riverbank. He was home and dry.
When he stopped watching, his regrets left on the tide.

Wrapped Wilderness

Soft sounds are natural. Only in their long absence
do we begin to understand that we are
finely weaved from the wrapped wilderness.
Last night, I dreamt I was a coil of grass

rope floating on the bay at tide change.
Below me was a current slowly turning inward
to a main river and tributaries of silence
in a noisy world. I was searching for a rift

where I could hang on to the bottom
of the bay with a piece of seaweed
to see who could soak the longest. I lost.
I was pulled straight upward by the blonde hair

of my youth. I was a new sound above a shadow at sunrise—
soft cries in the light, not the gravel-throated calls before black.
My morning became a cast-off gillnet from the land of the next.
I couldn't keep fog in my ears—I was only a guest.

Silt and Mud

Time is a log raft behind a smoking face.
It is a sight around the corner of a river
on a slip-and-fall summer day.

You don't hurry when you cut
through silt and mud. The log raft follows
the cast and reel. Boomsticks know where

shirts and shoes will gather next as people
turn the fish and travel faster than the current
and as slow as the wake of a felled tree.

Swell

In the fog, the outside is unpainted.
You weave a leg rope out of dry beach grass.
You're alive. You rode here on the creek
of your mind, down the base of a mountain

to a narrow valley of smoky sand. The distance
from who you must be to "get on" and "take care"
is only half listening. Waves hit the beach
and carry boots and booze full circle to

a sack of books. All the nets around you are left
on the shore. You're on the board. You catch a swell.
You yell, "Oh, hell!" and drop through the spices of the sky.
You rip outside the edges of logs, rocks, and debris.

Below the Surface

Below the surface of the water drags
an old gaff hook of good intention.
It's for gifts we wash off in the river
for the nets of our neighbor's front porches.

Up and down the lined trail of our history,
we holler, laugh heartily, and wave like a pack
of matches caught in the wind along a riverbank.
More times than we want to remember,

we have felt the steep angle of loss
from full moon tides. Too fast or too slow,
fate, probability, or misfortune wouldn't let us
get away from its teeth. You can't always

tip and move to the other side of the boat.
You get swamped, washed out, and caught
in traps of old stumps and root-coil.
Get tough or get carried into ocean waters.

Peel off the bark of your unhappiness.
You don't have to be camera-ready.
You have a chest full of fish.
You don't have to be lonely.

Abundance

In the Coos River Valley, meat is preserved
in the smoke of peeled alder.
Most use a brine and let it soak overnight.
A neighbor might say,

"here is a gift to hold the racks."
A tongue on a wetted thumbnail
paints the humidity. Abundance pulls herself
to the top of the smoker with a full swing

and a half smile. She digs her claws in below her
and unravels the first curls of smoke.
Outside, a few spare fish scales shine
six colors of a healthy garden.

The hours drift and the head of smoke nudges
the lone, sweet scent of the notched breeze.
Hunger gets full on the meat off the bone.
Light slides into roots and seeds.

I Cast the Sand

The coffee this morning adds a little time
to the new day. I hold my hand over the steam
to keep warm. I awoke on the same level as the drafts.
Here, above this forest, my toes are lodged in the rafters

of my true home. I slowly stretch back and forth like the tide.
I wear wedged shoes, one last sock, and a well-worn shirt.
Mutts get on. I need to gather one more handful
of the sand of time. Can chalk bless dirt?

I am present and in the moment. I hang on
with my losses to not fall off the last of my good fortune.
I don't know where I'll land next. I'll keep moving
through this broken hourglass. My dreams are for the night.

I watch an image of the sun rising in the east. I go west
and climb cliffs with wilder animals. On my right,
I see speckled light shining across the crests
of crevices and cracks. I cast the sand before me.

Two Birds

Two birds were dried leaves in the cold wind.
They hung over an LED sign pouring out undrunk dreams
from the sky. Sometimes, a place won't let you stay.
You have to fly toward a new light that holds

a little warmth. Stay too long, beaks might turn
into pursed lips. Words follow their tails and get dizzy.
It takes strength and courage not to become
a bird beard of wolves and coyotes.

When you survive, you can close shears and cut straight
with claws to shaded grasses, mushrooms, and mosses
to heal from the year's nicks and scratches as you learn
dreams are more than specks of light you catch in your eyes.

Remaining Light

You might find me on the north edge
of an Oregon coastal mountain range
with a westerly view into the remaining light
of my youth's exuberant wonder with the world.

My thoughts trail on the wind
through canyon walls down to a point
of gratitude. In the shade, you might see
some forgiveness running off the green mossy

rocks of my calmness. It's a narrow shoulder
and a crag-crossed creek. It runs parallel
with a little gulch through a tree line
of my belief that forgiveness and gratitude

aren't a couple of ripped rags
(with chunks of dirt on both sides) from an old,
rural, river valley with hillside gardens
full of good people who ebb and flow with the tides.

On the River We Float II

The river we float has a pace
beyond the town's prepared embrace,
as our untempered souls regale in
the submerged acknowledgments as life

awaits. The freckled shade of the shore's
willow, a welcoming gift accepted
as an invitation to the confirmation of our
meliorism—we are selected.

Returned to the throne beneath the sea,
archipelago of clearing water—
our spirits, like fish in a chase full of play
in the stream, we stay in motion as day

turns to veiled night, our memories
a keeper of history within the depths
of our body's own way. Currents
as lore—a pressing measure of time.

Freshets of joy in swirling binds,
the river ties delight the mind.
The tide-forged and river-hewed,
again, connections are old and new.

Selected Poems

Coos River Reverberations:
Poems of River, Farm & Forest (2021)

Amble: Poems (2021)

Idling Intuitions: Poems (2022)

Mast Years: Poems (2022)

Coos River Reverberations: Poems of River, Farm, and Forest (2021)

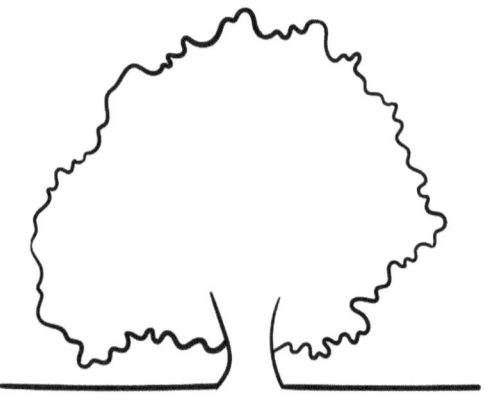

Tidal River Swimming Hole

Foam circles on top,
leaves drifting below,
back this way
in ten minutes or so.

No need to hurry,
let me commune
on this incoming tide
with no slack till noon.

Slow circle now,
I am spinning round,
just a few more loops
before heading to town?

Might as well tarry
with the afternoon breeze,
with the sea salt ions
through the grass and the leaves—

life repeats,
and it can soothe,
this time is for me—
my nature's truth.

Mr. Buzzard

Mr. Buzzaaard, you wily turkey vulture—
my old friend—as I look up,
right now to me, you are summer,
and even more so

when I was much younger.
In my youth, your flight did please.
Now older, you have become more offending—
a sort of death-pending breeze.

Up high in the air,
you float above the land and the seas,
up high in the air,
you selfishly glide to find

those with needs in final death pleas.
Still, you are a signal of my freedom
to run in the dry grass without shoes,
a pendulum of the seasons,

alive you pronounce,
confirm, and strangely bemuse.
Down along the river,
a long search, a short cruise—

no animal wasted,
no food too abused.
You seem to enjoy to fly in a circle
with your weathered traveling friends,

when not squaring off
with too many other vultures.
Always testing your lens,
you have a careful, long look,

you try to avoid trouble.
Is it easier for you
with your death-mimicking shuffle?
Not even in your youth,

do you appear as fresh as others in suckle.
Now older, the less harmless you appear—
a harbinger of death.
My summers are more dear.

No time for fear.
A little grass is still green.
I am still alive as you can see.
Watch me be me—run, laugh, and dream.

Night Swimming

Sudden summer night swimming,
means good times are brimming.
The star wind can be cool;
this river is warm like an old thermal pool.

Generally, a sandbar or dock
will support the echo
of gleeful splash shock.
But, underappreciated

in my personal view,
is the lack of water animals
who see me as chew.
Like all forested areas

one still must show care,
but few places in the world,
during summer seem so safe—
gratefully, the danger so rare.

No poisonous snakes
to swim with me,
nor below the water,
dangers from critters brew.

So, tonight I will swim free
from the willow-hugged riverbank,
in this small, open clearing
to wash the new-chanced sand

from between my safe toes.
With a fast, out-of-the-gate, running dive,
Doppler effect in full stride,
I will announce my arrival,

then after a leisurely and joyful stay,
I will let the full blue moon
lighthouse my way back
to the welcoming shore.

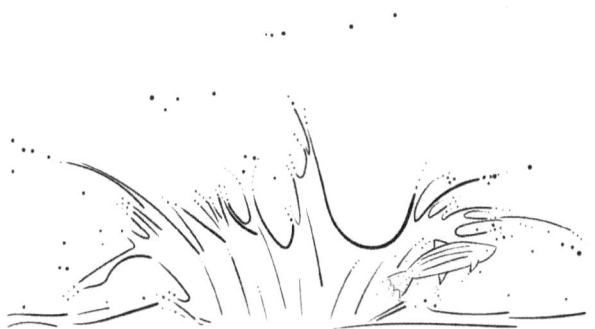

Stars

Away from town,
as the light goes to ground
I like to sit and quietly watch
the brightening stars.

The flap of an owl,
a far off strange small growl
the air moves across
my relaxed, careworn, old face.

The air I breathe in,
and my chest does ascend,
as my head and my eyes
move slightly tipped back.

Shimmer afar as my chair
sinks in the sandbar,
a sudden loud splash,
a squeal and a crash

cover the sound
of the ice rattling in my drink jar.
The night is alive with the chase,
our world is spinning on pace,

I find watching stars does imbue
the glory of the universe in view,
I am so lucky tonight
lets me life-hew.

Looking Out the Classroom Window

In the fall, while in high school,
I would look out the classroom window
at nature, the jewel, and I was obsessed.
Why was I going to practice again

on another sunny afternoon?
These training structures,
after a long day of class,
energizing for some, but draining for me.

I suppose I have always been called
to the land. An understandable attachment
for a happy, freedom-loving youth
who grew up next to what seemed

like his private, boundaryless, coastal mountain
range. I lived like an enterprising tinkerer,
and I seldom got bored,
yet for a competitive,

small-town youth,
testing myself against peers
was also always a calling so strong that
I chose to restrain my secure love of nature

to better help overcome my insecure sense
of self. And, for most of my life
that has been the dynamic,
but now that I am older,

the quieter voice to spend more time in nature
is almost the only voice I wish to hear,
and it keeps getting louder—
beckoning me home.

The hope I feel—
though not always constant—
is like an unexpectedly hiked upon
wild cherry blossom display of abundance—

full of numerous, uncountable blossoms,
yet somehow, the world never runs out of room.
I, like the land, am nurtured each day
by every bloom.

Afternoon Music Hour

When Grandfather retired,
much music he sired,
making my early afternoons
so full of good sound.

In summer, double front doors wide open—
piano notes floating breezily away as softly
as colorful, rhododendron flower scents.
A few songs in the queue,

ones he loved,
minded, and renewed.
The music, a centerline through his life,
and I suppose now mine,

as I reflect
how confident I feel when I am settled and still
as the notes help me keep a good temperament
and a more harmonious path.

This stringed life near the river, a siren to me—
playing light and secure—
this timing brings me back to full joy
and the life I have procured.

I am reminded in this present
moment that my life is
always enhanced and soothed
through these sounds,

so on this orienting afternoon,
may I also be a tuned-comfort
to my leisurely guests
and dear listening friends.

A Summer Home

No place quite so sweet,
as the summer river home you can keep,
though harder to find for most,
and an expensive way to host.

But, by work of the brow,
or inheritance trowel
the result is the same.
The place must be alight

with great sights that delight
all the senses to take your cares away.
So, a good place to start
is with flower seeds thrown in an arc

while remembering
to get those bulbs planted in the fall.
A few wildflower volunteers
can add to the cheer

on at least half an acre as course,
which will only add to the source
of splendor, mirth,
and contentment that abounds.

One must also take care
to remember to share,
for the wise always say
that a life of abundance

is enhanced by what good we give.
Not the paths to the absence of pain,
nor care to always find financial gain,
(though nice) is doing (that) much.

So, plant some bright
flowering shrubs
and fruit trees,
and make such a great idyllic scene

to lift the weight of the world
from your welcome guests
as well as help you live out a summer
of joy, leisure, and plentiful rest.

A Riverside Garden Work Party

Tilled with heavy, sweating brows,
forty yards long by ten yards wide,
I hope we have enough energy when we're done
to sow the crisscross pattern in fine lines.

The sandy old pine soil tastes bittersweet,
the rototiller has made it
all barrel-waved rows and ecstatically neat.
So tempting for the deer, this future resplendent,

fresh and crunchy contained treat,
that we must now build the deer fence,
and not feel bad that out of Nature's gate,
such a bundled cornucopia

they never would meet.
This garden will bring
canning and dry store planning
to be added to our smoking and broaching,

which means that friends and family
will more likely have something ripe
through abundant planting,
not unfortunate poaching.

A garden valley we are in—
cloistered, salty bay breezed, wild flowered,
with surprisingly myrtle-scented bees.
After work, sweat-laden and dry soil coated,

we will shake off the dust of dried clay
and pull a cold beer out of the fridge
or a neat, olive-stirred "nifter" off the tray.
We will get ready to eat some of last year's

harvest of the day,
and share some irreverent laughs
and good chatter as we recount the refreshing,
yet odorous and cooling wind off the river—

blown from the bi-monthly, minus tide,
heavily impacted Coos Bay.
When dinner is ready
and all is put away,

our energy lagging
and hearts full of play,
talking may lull,
but let our love never sway.

Homemade Smoker

A smokehouse was built right
from cedar siding built tight,
four feet wide, three feet deep,
and six feet high. Inside, six sturdy metal racks

all laid level and straight,
and fed by a dirt-covered tunnel,
metal barrel cut lengthwise as a fire plate.
Many fighting shad were hit by smoke,

bones so soft not to choke—
oh, such harvesting fun did the fish provoke,
even more fun to catch than smallmouth bass per stroke,
if not in every heavy-sounding strike on the fishing pole,

then each potent early-summer flash of memory
of the reaffirming river churning from abundant schooling,
past the ready, fishing boats and the sturdy, welcoming dock—
paired with frothy, boisterous, and occasionally tipsy,

long echoing friendship toasts of times past,
sometimes forgotten in this busy world,
but loved by many, again recorded, and preserved to last.
Spring and fall Chinook salmon too,

were brought through the long smoke
while courses of striped bass
(for a few years) came through en masse.
As we opened the door,

smoke would waft from ceiling to floor
causing a choking, big watering-eyed step back,
and we would look giddily
at all the fish on each rack—

fish scales all removed,
the skin stuck and improved
was now nature's perfect raft
and so ready to graft

before taking it back to the house;
great care was always taken
not to overconsume on the first swoon.
The pantry was always ensured to have space,

for the joy of seeing a wall of canned jars
in the winter, is a kind of warmth and grace
experienced most finely by the grateful—
in a well-stocked and run place.

Salmon on the Fire Pit

What can be better than to sit by the fire,
with a circle of chairs full of friends
you admire. You don't have to wait to retire.
Of course, sitting alone can be a good thing to do,

but better it seems to view with your crew.
Sandstones all around
to gravel the ground,
a fire pit was made from clay

for this place to astound.
In late fall and early spring,
fillets of salmon I was happy to bring—
open with care to prepare for good fare

of parsley, garlic, and lemon on a bed of butter
with a steady sear of the meat,
then skin side until neat—
barbequed thirty-five

to forty-five minutes over hot coals.
As a child, I ate so much salmon it would seem,
that it was not until I was five in dog years
I was again keen to eat my plate clean.

Yet, the unapologetic fun we did sow.
The conversation would flow.
With an empty plate, dark and late,
we would stare at the stars and our fate.

Gone Too Soon

I feel your pressed hand upon my shoulder,
I don't have you, yet I must get older.
Since you have left this land, I must be bolder.
What shall I do with my new child and new life?

On the eve of the end of our strife,
my valued father is gone.
We thought we had twenty more years with you.
The room is quiet, weight sinking, I feel blue—

can anything here ever lift my bleak review?
We fought, we talked, you guided me through,
but I still had so many vital questions to ask—
so many stories to hear of your past.

(I was still young), our time did not last.
Older now . . . even than you,
would you be proud
of what I have made it through?

You're a grandfather. I wish you knew.
I am still a tempestuous man from time to time.
It must be hardwired. It's helped on the land.
I think it is tied to my high tolerance of pain—

I like to believe it helped
as a genetic, loving, keep-on-living gift
I carry from you.
I wonder now, what unfinished business

you felt you had left,
a life for some,
just over half met.
While my race is further along,

there are always some things left to do,
I suppose fewer now,
but I am older now than you.
I like to believe you were as content then as I am now.

I am so happy to know I was wrong
when I thought our time would not last,
since love, rich memories, and discovered stories
keep you alive somehow

and help me hold to you,
not just staying in the past,
but moving both steadily forward
and caringly through.

Barbed Wire

Old leather gloves
and wound metal of barbed wire,
dry my sweating hands
from nicks and new scars' ire;
let this western redcedar fence post

brace tighten after I wind
this last stick of myrtle.
Some wonder why I often rework
this unemployed fence,
I have no cattle now,

but this is the only way life makes sense.
Get me out early,
see my rising warm breath,
pour from my thermos—
I will take care of the rest.

Four more braces to build,
one more log to peel—
I have got old leather gloves
and wound barbed metal to feel.
I may complete the fences quickly

or take all year,
if they do not work as well as I planned,
I will tear them down and move them,
but I will still keep them in my sphere.
I need to keep moving to run far away

from disappointed thoughts
of regret, remorse, and delay;
sometimes, I work headlong for a sense of control
with a desire to share beauty and order.
I work on this old,

unprofitable farmland
to help my family, friends, and neighbors
to feel that so far out here,
we can still somehow
make it stay maintained,

improved, efficient, and conformed.
But, this land always grows
and tends to confound,
so it challenges and makes my past work omissions,
lack of time or money redound.

I will wake up tomorrow,
and I will most likely rework
another unemployed fence—
I have no cattle now,
but this is the only way life makes sense.

Outworked

I always thought myself of care,
so hard work I ventured,
without much despair,
yet never in all my days,

was I able to keep up
with my father's work ways.
On the day you know you are strong,
imagine if you kept that feeling lifelong

with each job a challenge to test your might,
each work party task
a sort of melee night fight.
As an adult, I marvel still

at fence posts dug in degrees of thrill
and trucks of firewood filled double strokes,
left throw, now right—hurry now, let's go!
Who needs sports,

when living with work so grand?
For me, all the following events
have seemed too pretentious and canned.
You have to be adept to play against nature

the chance player as well the stage—
who competes with calculated gait
in the long, great game of health against age.
When we tire, or our attention is strained,

it slowly takes our victories
and laughs heartily at all our gains.
I will remember the extreme work
put out on the many days,

appreciate the many trials,
and wish hospitably others who might come late
to take over what has been our ways—
may they enjoy the game,

all the wins and all the play—
given they do not ignorantly flout or discount
the hard-earned accomplishments
of my father's work ways.

The Windstorm

Candles set out,
racing-like wind song
moves fluidly and stout.
A raking alongside the house,

and only strong branches will sojourn
before finding company in creeks and puddles
also adorned with leaves,
mud, and long-past sticks,

as the gusty whooshing comes,
swirling heavily tonight, then it runs.
How much can these windows bear?
That tree was too near, why did I not shear?

Oh, that broken treetop on the far hill,
almost had its own will.
Warm in the house now,
maybe take my bow,

I think, early to bed for me.
When the power goes,
better to be in bed with comfy toes;
perchance not a better place to enjoy

an old-fashioned
woodstove low-glow night,
all the world will seem right.
Frozen pipes are a fright,

the faucet is not tight,
but a fire I will want to be built
better tonight, a morning with no guilt.
The extra water jugs are now full,

the teapot on the wood stove
should help calm tomorrow's lull.
Tired now, a melodic yawn,
sleep I'll enter until the dawn.

Blue Smoke Around the Card Table

In the time of my youth,
I heard many a rebuke,
on my sensitivity to smoke at my booth.
Were my tears for my card hand,

or the blue air that was fanned?
Certainly, move or be damned.
Around the old, yet lively game table,
a few adults were quite health-loving and stable,

but a few expressively
waived wide their hands through the air
like both a low-lit cave torch and a rusted, flaking saber.
Though we now deeply know

that cigarette smoke,
is like inhaling time-released death strokes—
hopefully, in my case, over time,
it is cured by red wine and fun folks.

Strangely, still, sometimes
I even crave the social blue fog of war,
with even negative smell remembrances
deep in mind or on the fore,

smoke-covered clothing,
red eyes, yet seemingly for many
it is now just lore.
But, oh the good

tear-jerk, raucous laughs
that were had,
somehow make it all
so much bigger than life and not so bad.

Like shad on the river,
time makes all things a fad.
As an adult,
what I would not sometimes give and do,

to be back playing again
in that era and hue—
I would have one more day
to see you all through the blue.

Cow Jam

My first word as a child was *cow*.
At five o'clock,
twice each-and-every day,
some fifty-five cows, or more,
would pass my way,

one hundred yards back from the gray gravel
and manure-spackled country road,
I sometimes looked through
the front house windows
as they slowly passed my parent's abode.

A sound click and a clack,
a quick, sweet-stolen stop
for some fresh grass,
with a hand pat from the farmer
and barks from the dogs,

the cows would reflexively dash,
then return to measured moving
along to the fields.
My parents told me,
the farmer was needed

with his dogs and his family
to protect those cows
from getting lost on their way
from day-fields to night-hills,
and back again each day.

In return, the cows did relay—
circular-shaped, past-feed
for neighbors to circuitously dodge
on their rounds to town
and milk—the fruit of present and future hay,

which allowed the farmers to be paid.
All, so the farmer, his dogs, and his family
could afford to continue that way of life
to walk those fifty-five, easily-lost-cows,
past my parent's driveway,

at five o'clock,
twice each-and-every day,
seven days a week,
so 365 days per year.
Now older,

whenever I start to feel burned out,
fatigued, irritated by routine,
or not sure where in life I am going,
I often remember that good farmer
with his dogs and his family, and I think:

—*Routine*, what am I complaining about?
There are days too when I am
sitting and looking out my front window
(no longer on the farm)
and a mail carrier passes my way,

at approximately the same time
each-and-every day,
and I immediately think of the cow jam.
I then start feeling nostalgic
as I remember drinking

cows' milk fresh from the dairy,
or hearing cow hooves echoing
with a hollow and soothing click and clack
off the river road through the valley,
and even strangely enough,

the often tedious,
summer afternoon washing
of fresh cow manure off my parent's cars.
Today, when I think back,
I can so easily hear and see

that procession of cows where I grew up,
and the farmer with his dogs, and his family,
keeping those cows on their way,
and I am grateful. I think to myself:
I love those farmers—

(click) they helped me find my first word,
(clack) they let me feed the calves bottles,
(click) they let me scoop the grain in the loft,
(clack) and play in the milk barn,
(click) and spend time with them and their animals.

So, my first word was *cow,*
and I finally realize that the farmer
with his dogs and his family
kept more than cows
on that country road from getting lost.

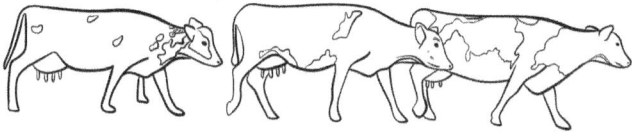

Himalayan Blackberry

Considered a berry,
but really an aggregate fruit,
in short—good to eat,
but hard to treat.

Once cultivated, but now on the run,
a challenge to have a go,
only thorn-slowed by a mow,
so most decide to use

herbicide with a good sticker,
but digging up will also suffice.
Born in the cradle,
with the mind of a ladle,

it made its way
to live free as a wild crop.
Many people value the taste,
but I suspect those who own land,

which Himalayan blackberries embrace,
deep in their soul, feel a bit more chaste—
for this damn fruit has no limit to growth.
How much over the years has been spent,

on poison poured with no sustained dent?
If more effective options were found,
I could invest the money locally,
in better helping my family and friends,

instead of spraying questionable chemicals
as my maintenance account money goes down
and a corporation's dividend payments go up.
So, what can I do to save the fields?

I hope the answer is not to give up and
buy and hold chemical company mutual funds.
(I am too stubborn and affected, I guess).
I hear Tansy Ragwort is now under control;

can we retrain the underemployed
cinnabar moth, flea beetle, and seed head fly?
The Himalayan blackberry is out of hand—
I will give almost anything new a try to free the land.

Woodstove in the Old Ranch House

In fall, winter, and early spring,
gray plumes of smoke
sometimes twist and wring,
so for fun in the home,

we sit by the stove,
fully embraced and heated
in a peaceful trove.
How many fires, has this home seen?

How many mires, this home gave lean?
A crackle here, a sudden pitch pop, the scent of alder,
all in a shot; many days I have been away,
in my mind's eye, this day I sought.

Oh, give me days of heavy rain,
send me waves of levy wane, so in this place
I may unhurriedly enjoy a healing, Finnish heat,
a warm reminder of life's kinder feat.

Born in this valley
or come here freight—
know we are gifted now—
let our cares abate.

To Town

Some go every day
to get a sweet treat,
while others hunker way down
as if on retreat;

I tend to think that the type of "riverite"
you are, does not matter at all,
since both come from a place
of more privacy and fresh trees that are tall.

They come from a place
not always easy and fair,
so they travel with a hardiness,
good instincts, and great care,

since robustness it takes
to live so far from the gates of the town
with a particular steeliness driving straight
along the river road to not drown,

but it is hard to expect
to live there long all alone
when the country calls out
for you to eventually atone,

so connect with your neighbors
and offer a favor,
they will be sure
to do the same for you.

Cookies at holidays,
or mow a little more of the shared road,
drop off some stitching, or a regional,
heartfelt, poetry book ode.

A Walk Up the Draw to Recharge

Summer lends to jaunty bends,
and I am called to walk up the draw.
A reverberant call to roam amidst the loam—
every time I feel I am home.
How many have felt the same?

Now running, climbing, jumping, stumping—
here at this moment, life is thumping—
and I feel alive and healthy,
never so wealthy,
for what do I work for if not for this?

What few life-cares were even brought,
a break shall make for naught,
with my dwindling public awareness.
So, along this course,
I will keep walking deep

in this creek to find the source.
Here, true nature is the feature,
and privacy is the teacher,
may it find me a worthy creature.
I know by heart the refrain,

never fall in love with the farm,
nothing more can be gained,
and it usually will just end in harm.
Love is not reason,
no matter the season,

and sometimes the land chooses you.
I must limit my expenses,
and take care of the fences,
while mending the hives
and harvesting the honey,

which helps me build
multiple increasingly passive revenues
(limited goods they may be),
working toward them is still my life's chosen dues.
All while I pursue

the old path to glory in any age
of working a little good each day
to keep a purpose and in motion,
for the day will surely come,
when my body is undone,

and I will likely have to move away,
so I will sit in this fortuitous moment,
and I shall savor and own it,
knowing heaven on earth,
for me, is in this brief bestowment.

When I Grow Up

In the Coos River Valley, put out your hand
and you are likely to touch a tree,
if you keep your hand on for long,
the advice may come free.
When I was young, I lived in the now,

but by eight, I often wondered about my fate.
On a contemplative walk,
during an afternoon dawdle with life,
I once set the palm of my hand
open touching on an old, woodpecker-holed

and rock-rough to the touch, volunteer pear tree.
Suddenly, many professions
flashed through my mind
and it told me all the things
I would not grow to be,

which was so strange
that my hand reflexively pulled away,
and I felt stung by a combination
of loss, regret, stinging nettle, and bee—
it was stark and apparent, even as a child,

I experienced something spiritual,
maybe few ever see.
I left the forest sometime later,
with fewer work options
and even more questions.

None more on my mind
than if this all meant I would die young,
or if this tree was saying, more hopefully,
a heart-matched profession
was in the future, yet to be.

As I got a little older, I often reflected back
on my experience with the forest presence of
seemingly potent mystery and knowledge
that gave me for an instant a third eye
to see history without haulage.

Though grateful to have made
it out of childhood alive,
I was still left figuring out my life's big
question: all the remaining things I would grow to be.
I was feeling the pull of that twisted vision,

of an intriguing future deep in my being,
but I could see no correlation
to my current actions, for the fruits of gifted
subtractive knowledge still leaves much to see.
I felt this forsakenly, even immaturely,

on my extended amble between
unsatisfying jobs, lost loves, and too much taking
from others while trying to figure life out,
I was never quite wholly free of the day
I came across that old tree, even while walking

in a healing canyon or paddling on a river
to the mountain or the sea.
The weekend before I finally moved
from home, while out cutting a few
dead firewood trees for my parents,

I ventured into that old,
hollow, and slowly departing,
myrtle grove, I never came to alone,
and I finally sought out
that volunteer, long-past pear maker,

seemingly childhood haunter
and planter of seeds of confusion,
over-reflection, and doubt.
It was almost leafless then, punky, yet
surprisingly strong. I angrily raised

my ax to the hollow trunk
to finally be done with it,
but at that moment, I finally felt free,
so I placed my hand palm open upon it,
once again, feeling as if this time,

that was where it was supposed to be,
and for just an instant, I thought it again spoke to me.
Startled and excited, I prepared then and there
to have my future settled
and the full meaning finally gleaned,

yet this time, I sensed no pain,
and when I listened, felt, and saw nothing.
Only observant nature greeted me.
Now that I am much older and better traveled,
unsteadily careered, and dreaming to be bolder,

I still walk the forest where that old pear tree used to be,
and I wonder—was that time nothing but a child's first
self-awareness smolder? The days are colder.
I hope there is still time to believe it is a sign.
My dreams are getting older.

Chittum Bark

To make a few bucks in spring to early summer
I used to help take my grandfather's truck
to fill the bed high with Chittum bark,
and only a pocketknife was often used

to cut from the base to the top without an ark.
The pay was not great
for such piecemeal work in the stand,
but all said, I was not so rich

as a child to not give it a hand.
The smell of the bark,
made the knowledge quite stark,
and I was reminded again—

like so many times before—
that making money on a lark
is most often not a walk in the park,
and speaking of a lark,

did its use when applied to fingers
ever help people
not to bite their fingernails?
As work though, it was better than some activities

I could have been doing as I suppose there were a few
people around who were not so honest and true
to make bread by the sweat of their brow—
who the hell buys Chittum bark anyway?

Maybe they know better—currency is only real if it can be torn.
In the end, this was just one false start,
and indeed, financially off the mark,
yet it has become part of the fun youth in my heart.

Maple Leaves Piled in the Dry Creek Bed

Early fall in the canyon—
dry, empty creek beds bridged
with maple leaves by the armloads—
the warlike trenches packed with yesterday's sun,

tomorrow's dirt, and the day's energy.
On our bikes, we'd hop
off the ramp with a glide-drop,
a soft landing—the goal for the day.

Ending wet-matted and tattered,
but like the leaves—thoroughly used up, by hard play.
The climb out was a bit of a slippery ascent,
so strong muscles were needed for prolonged reaching

toward snapping roots and short dirt-hold grips,
and it is funny to me that I do not remember
thoughts about hitting protruding rocks
or a creek's edge.

Maybe it's not surprising for kids full of unfettered days
and no parents near, with the only real fear
being that the day would go way too quickly
before it was time for big meals of good cheer.

Today, I still get such a bolt,
when the leaves on the trees turn yellow
and fall to the ground where I live.
Though I'm too old now to have a second go.

I offer a smiling embrace to those who know,
when I think back to those days
full of all the new seasons' joy
and all the fearless, free-falling flow.

Myrtle Grove

A slippery lot,
leaves beneath the tree knots,
so I try not to slide down the hill.
Thick is the floor,
with nature's galore,

so prolific is this forest duff,
but no matter how many,
room for more penny-colored leaves.
I wave my hands through blue, greenish-gray moss,
of fine dangling tree reams of time and loss,

a creaking warily sound, a snap may abound,
If the wind picks up in the afternoon.
Dark and clean is the scene,
everywhere in between under the canopy
in this pleasantly covered,

once temple moor made hollow rune.
Cleanse my worldly cares,
let go of despair,
this place is where I can just be,
for how else to explain,

the release of my pain,
in this shelter from trauma and care.
My journey was long,
here I belong,
as I look at the river through the trees,

seeing birds in the air, showing little care,
as they ride gusty winds
through embracing air pockets
in the sky above me.
This ground has been protected

from most of the evils, I fled,
naïve it is not, as all deep time is fraught.
It too has seen dreams come to naught.
Its first people forced to move
after a long, spirit-filled, and symbiotic stay,

and knowing its part in the era,
it still mourns in its way.
It, too, knows my ancestor's loss and pain
and it shall wash with the rain
only some of our joined hurt, anger,

and remorse away. Listen, it is calling,
all nature is falling
in rhythm like these heavy,
slow dripping, raindrop-ridden leaves.
So infrequently these days,

I don't seem to hear anything
beyond my next fear,
if only I would, I might get back some
of my energy and genuine desire for health gains.
I breathe deeply and exhale any need for constant grit,

tense my muscles and release buried stress—
hoping once again my mind will finally return fit.
I do not need to visualize a relaxing place to be,
for wholeness is the essence of this grove of old trees
full of silence, serenity, and the forefather of keys.

Living Near the Stream

Weather wrought, soil gained,
roots were loosened in the rain.
A tree was brought down during the night,
the road is open now but with a fight.

Looks like it is late to work once again
after heading back to the house
to shower and change,
since now a dress shirt and pants,

maybe a blouse,
are covered in—woodchips,
dirt, bar oil, gas, and the rain,
but today, you are the hero neighbor,

the chosen one,
who gets to remember that our river road
is mostly—clean, maintained,
partially paved and graveled,

which happens to be located
in a coastal mountain range,
with a temperate rainforest climate
full of neighbors the whole way

with occasionally, untimely falling trees.
Oh, one more thing—
for the good deed of
using your very own chainsaw,

so others could drive through,
and you so quickly placed it in the back,
of your once-clean,
but now dirty—car, truck, or SUV,

it too is full of sawdust, sticking in a ream,
and will need to be cleaned
as a meditative practice,
I like to call—*living near the stream.*

Froze Last Night

Awake with a quiver,
my body in a shiver,
did it snow so early
in the canyon this fall?

No, just a deep glossy frost,
and the grass is awash
as white as the freshly driven snow,
so I must tramp around,

chores do abound— oh, how I love to see
my footprints left on the ground.
Like a beautiful old map,
full of dashes like a double-headed crossed ax

(as I look back) this way and that I went,
the ground is a crunch, today at least until lunch—
better tighten my jacket and pull down my warm hat.
This day is for me, and I am so full of glee,

I get to live out in these woods.
Never so sweet is the joy
that comes from the bad which we beat—
escaping the city is grand,

so I will walk up the hill, just for the thrill
to let my breath feed these great trees,
my lungs and these pine reverse and achieve
a harmony so good for the soul.

Made for each other, this frost will not forfeit
but only enhance and bring sight to our kinship.
In these last minutes of the morning,
let us offer each other our shared gifts as life unfolds.

Dusk

Heavy eyes of rods, more light comes in,
slowing now, the day is dim.
Deer wander by, none I care to keep—
they will make it safe through
tonight's sweet sleep.

The fountain of light has spun away,
evening lulls without delay.
My blessings, pains, and complex thoughts
are invited now to quieter spots.
A comforting form to take to sleep—

candlelit rhyme resounding through blinks.
No matter the outcome, all I can say,
not all were so lucky on this day.
Less than a flutter in what is time—
infinite existence or just a line.

Amble: Poems (2021)

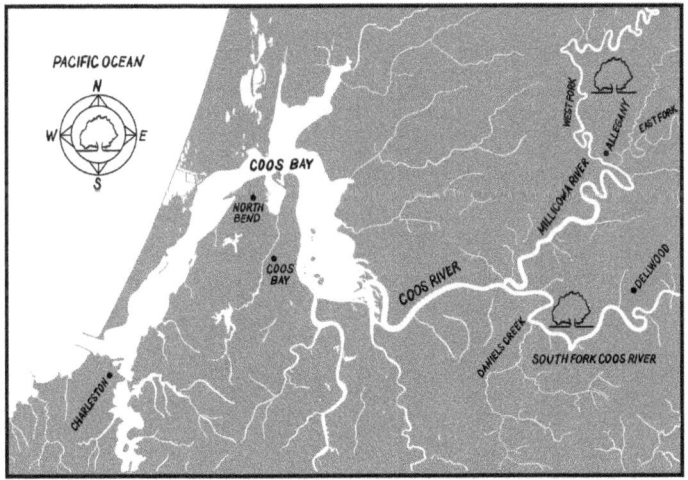

COOS RIVER VALLEY, OREGON

Amble

I took three walks on my first trip back in three months.
Three glorious excursions where I ambled so slowly,
they may qualify as the same walk. I had moments of bliss
in the canyon so fine that I almost dug a hole with my hands
to bury my body in the earth and fall into the sleep of myrtles
to live three hundred years and survive three major fires to
record in my rings. I measured strikes of lightning nearby
in uprooted trees. All around, I found old sounds stored in
broken crowns. Tree survival after lightning is not all
by chance. All living creatures have an evolved and buried sense
of humor. Dead trees like bones are hollow conductors of energy
as worn electric strands. I shed my fears like trees shed leaves
in laughter. I am home. I was wrong. Even if I don't live here,
my ambles affirm my promise—I belong. I belong. I belong.

When We Help

Moving that wood was a little more challenging this year.
The same goes for the brush clearing near the house,
which even for me at my age is a hard clear and a long sweat.
You are still at it with most of the work, as it is with you,
through near misses and health-defying chances.
It felt like we pushed the rusted hinges harder this year.
This place is beautiful and such a hammock-infused joy.
If not here forever, where do you want to be?
The answer might quicken the final projects.
You can enjoy the focused work of a younger neighbor.
Our proximity, our bond—we work in this valley, clear-eyed.
You made the mantle to pass in this mountain and garden
valley. When you leave this land, what you love lives on
through the landscapes we shaped and the promises I keep.

Measure of Loss

I see where to end up.
I have lived away and fought to secure my future stay.
I might have even more fear than before.
The talented and fearful ones who leave arrive late.
The talented and brave, who stay, often better know
the truth of good fortune—the place you love is an answer.
All the questions of why are a measure of your loss.
Today is a new day. What might I bring back
from my time away? Can I call it a sabbatical,
slow travel, helping the family? Halve it? Split an excuse
down the middle? Take my need or want and go? Will I live
to remember the monumented sky and know it was more
than the reflection of other people's poems in the back of my eyes?
I see where to end up. It has fewer regrets and whole sighs.

Fox Gloves

Pink, purple, yellow, and white whales
on the hill swimming
in yesterday's seas.
The silent bells of spring.
Each flower is a thimble
to turn each season gently like pages.
Poisonous to stay palatial.
Sentinel to succor a tomorrow.
A cresting call to sound an invitation
to the day's more watchful sky.
A child's fleet of starships
and a parent's lone burial crown.
A model foundation to becoming.
Spring's favorite plant to grow in broken light.

Broadleaf Dock

Perennial as the grass and opportunistically reproducing
mainly by seed (like other coastal inhabitants),
it prefers to make its way in the world in wet and poorly drained
areas. A large mound of foliage is its settled plumage of display.
Rosette-shaped spirit, contemplative, and durable.
Densely packed like its hopes, yet terminal
primarily focused on living and growing undisturbed.
Mature, even flowering in rust-colored panicles.
Brown in the winter—a root's favorite color.
Like other locals, as commonly found in fields,
meadows, and pastures—exceptionally pleased
when things are settled and comfortable.
As constant as sand forming sandstone.
There is freedom where it can grow.

Infused Path

The path between our homes is a pleasant walk
while heading to an early, still dark-skied,
kitchen-table-holding, hot cup of light
coffee and sometimes, surprisingly,
homemade dandelion and mint tea.
I think it is my late morning return home
on the narrow, forest-river-infused path
with the sun shining my way
from your home to mine, that I am
most aware and grateful we chose
to live next to each other, rarely ever needing
to drive, and even when walking
far away,
never leaving home.

Potted Oregon Myrtle

I grow potted myrtle tree starts to quell missing home.
I capture and release them as gifts to my friends—
those with hearts left near the bay. I crumble a leaf to inhale
a connection to a peppery, camphoraceous note. My thoughts
travel like old leaves on the breeze. I fly above thirst and hunger.
The sky was given as a reflection of the ocean without nets.
I seek joy and community as I water the present and amend
the soil of lost years. I get by. I grow the seeds for a food
the world doesn't know it requires. I borrow a belief from Bonsai.
Freedom is contained and sheared out of license.
A concept that is as hard-earned as it is as lightly understood.
In each generation, the world is a beguiling place.
Where does a bird fly next when its nest cannot be replaced?
Not every cry sheds a tear. Deep roots move through space.

On the Mountain

Who is the hermit on the mountain?
Are his sounds too light to hear?
The rustling of fabric as he tends the fire—steady, short steps, layered with the slight crunching of the duff forest floor beneath the earth-kissed soles of his feet. Much like the soft sounds of the world's once roar—peppered, crackling, blended, yet so muffled and distant, now, seemingly nothing more than silence after a final soft snapping ember's call as spent fuel to its flame. It is early morning, still dark, and the sun will not rise for a long while. The coals will persist, but only as a soft charcoal to find space, where a warm, healing heat was felt. Last night, I heard his voice in the wind. When I went to see him today, I saw an unburned root near the fire's edge, a new start, for an old trust in living. I thought of him—may the wiser wind stir the dust.

Moss Over Wood Ash

In temperate, Pacific Northwest rainforests, old, round,
ashed brush piles grow over. First, not with grass or weeds,
but with yellow and green moss—soft, comforting,
and rug-like. They must have once been appreciated
anciently by the spiritually attuned. In that instant—
the center of the universe. By their circular shape—
a vector for the eyes of the moon. In their silence—a setting
to absorb soundly orange sighs of the sun. Each year,
I clear a spot in the woods and burn my next brush pile,
knowing once again that the ash will climb away to a sky
it will shape. Moss grows over wood ash. Another year is
muffled rain. Soil is memory. Buried, latent answers seed
tomorrow's health. My questions overflow with the rain as I
sit and release my pain. Another year, what's been gained?

Summer Reflection

Today, I saw an attractive image shine brightly
off the water, the warm light reminded me of you,
full of joy and mirth. I could have sworn it was complete
with all the love you once had for me.
It was summer, an evening reflection,
just slightly out of reach, hopeful,
reminding me of the time we discovered
all of the untrammeled clovers on the side of that old,
cat-logged road, and felt confident
that somehow by doing so,
we must have already found the location
of our good fortune—the one we then quickly lost.
The unbroken-hearted cannot fairly value
whether a first love will be as sweet as the rest.

Bouquet of Nettles

I often take my chances with the nettles on my calves
and the stings on my arms—small, often
painful reminders that necessary motion
through even beautiful spaces are memorably
protected by both nature and what cannot be defined.
I find little comfort as I disturb the silence
of misty mornings or the light sounds
of the shedding dusk,
never comfortable as I find life in front of me,
its energies toward living another day, and mine
to deliver freedom from decline, hunger, and obscurity—
the price set by the unflavored ingredient of harvest,
together, part of the bouquet of production
for a tea to be born.

I Long for the Rain

I long for the rain as one more day finds me
covered, waterproofed, and pitter-pattered
from the first light until my coffee turns cold.
My steps are my part in the day's rhythmic sounding
down the river road and up
to the branches to songs in flight.
I walk the worn, damp clay paths that lead
to moss-covered, old burnt brush pile
views I clear each night for my mind.
I am upstream from my parent's collective loss.
I am infused with the spirit of life—play, love, and hope.
Have I kept the path clear for those who will come after?
I touch a misted alder leaf. A limb points to where it will
keep the grass asleep. I see five colors of fall. I cope.

Oregon Myrtle Trees

After the rain, Oregon myrtle trees stand wide, web-barked,
glistening. The breeze is infused with their evolving nature.
Their leaves release an airborne oil of clarifying expression.
The touch of the bark is a big, friendly rub
on the head of an aged, muscled, dust-covered bull.
If you touch them with patience, you sense them leaving.
We are just a passing leaf above roots too old to care.
Their expanding walls of thin bark show that nature knows—
even as we become more substantial, we stretch hollow inside.
They are the crack in the veneer between life and decline.
A living shell of our perceptions, as beautiful as their departing
leaves, which subtly change color in a mixed array.
The old know—not every figured eye at dusk will see
rust colored leaves fall in the unshaped dawn.

A Stop at the Dock

I like to break up my goings from here to there.
At the dock, I watch the water pass by me as the tide carries
the long-traveled sticks, forgotten fallen leaves,
and my buried, yet altered dreams to the bay.
I hear in the wind—*go where you go and with my goodwill.*
I remember the channeled, water-kissed air has a song
that holds me. I am called to share my weight to the balance.
My old hands no longer accurately measure what they can't hold.
Each day moves more of my intention. A child of place.
A spirit moves past me. A water-embraced recognition.
An inheritance fulfilled—a damp, sandstone path to a 7th generation.
One needed on the land with an arm full of firewood to keep warm.
A youth's seasonal awareness and an adult's seasoned sense to
know when to grow with the land or follow the water where it flows.

Idling Intuitions: Poems (2022)

Travel Without Touring

As the tractor shook, I thought:
"Engines at idle are still active."
The first answer that made sense
To me why there
Is not a more pronounced difference
In goodness between the curious young
Who travel and the curious young
Who stay home. Maybe elite private
Schools have the statistics on who
Improves most. I imagine it has
Less to do with where one
Goes and more to do with
Where one leaves. All things being
Equal, if it helps a youth
Thrive, travel seems the way forward
To a full and enriched odyssey
Of varied thoughts and telling tapestries.
Can my mind travel without touring?
I was the obligated and reverent
One who stayed. I needed more
Time to elevate what was before
Me. I care about other areas.
I'm old now, I rarely left
Home. I traveled through five generations
Of ancestors. I am them now.
Will future generations travel through me?

Arrived

When you arrived—your new home—
How much did you make it
Like your old? Did you choose
A similar climate, with the summer
Wind? This land that almost held
You like when you were young,
Outside in nature, did you travel
Back to the beginning? I am
Your ancestor. I do not see
The fates, nor feel the fibers
As you possibly remember. I don't
Hear your homeland speaking to me
About how I might return someday.
All I taste is the air
I cannot breathe when I imagine
Not being here, where you saved
The family. I know love, loss,
And, a tie to this land.
Because of you, if I returned
Back to your homeland, I might
Not see how to live easily
Without the scent of Oregon myrtle
Trees, alder shade, and western redcedar
Colors of the season full of summer
Flavors. I would miss the scents
In the river fields where flowing
Grass grows through sandy loam dirt
Ground deep below the old sea.

Some say to leave the home
I have known, should I believe
This land's peace will always follow
The generations who know the stories
And keep the subtle attachments maintained?
Given enough time, I am told,
The new wilderness becomes the old
Village. I say your daily prayer—
May all trails lead to home.

Patience

Waiting is another name for *time*.
Patience was the first idea after
Creation. All ideas can be wholly
Discovered in the mind that knows
Spirit is more than a mixture of earth
And what is grown. Life becomes
Wrapped in a shell to protect
What may be before a response
And ahead of what comes after.
The spring sets to share summer
Peace, joy, and rest in the promise
That everything is as it should
Be. Persevering life is not meager
In any meaningful and measured way.

Tolerance

Love is not the only law
Capable of helping people more humanely
Live well together. History has shown,
Good neighbors do not always love
Time together. Sometimes we must yell
No. Even when preferring to whisper
Yes. We hope for a consensus.
The views we hold can change
Over our lifetimes. We may reverse
Opinions we have securely held reverently
Through the many years of tradition.
Tolerance is an idea that arrives
After we understand that even unbalanced
Conversation is concretely preferable to conforming
Our beliefs with others' new definitions
Of belonging. Even more equitable words
Born of a thoughtful, universal design
Can be misapplied injuriously when stolen
From the tested. When new thoughts
Are modeled to replace warm reason
With cold, measured, demonstrated differences, only
Power changes direction. An hourglass isn't new
When it is flipped over. Filtered
Sand of the same size and shade
Is a tale of the trenches.

Ways Once Lived

The prepared practice of heavy provisioning
Gains with the gathering of family
And friends who frequent the festivities
Each year and work to alleviate
The burdens of the communal body
And mind. Full shelves, now emptier,
Mark that close cousins are fewer
And farther away in new areas,
And friends are elsewhere now helping
Their closer loved ones in need.
Memories bring forward the bittersweet
Understanding that you may be the last
Remaining to remember the boisterous laughs
Escaped, voiced with past hurts lightly
Healed over with time, and tenderly
Faced through ways once lived together.

Mast Years: Poems (2022)

Stories of Home

Stories sow into you. The people
With a shared vision of home
As a place of purpose that exists
Even after the land is gone.
For the sake of the children
The exiled seek new dawns. Away
From the long line of ancestors
From one place, with one heart,
The new land somehow seems less
Consequential. The water and the earth
Of the new land feels different
From old grounds that helped grow
The family. The stories of home
Are maps to places others own.
When I remember how I travel
Each day past cherished memories adapted
To fit my newfound understanding,
I try to leave more room
In my belief for better days
Ahead. Abundant days may arrive again
Brightening prospects to gather the gains
I can lightly and colorfully enjoy
Communally. The best stories graft past
Ways to celebrate what is cyclical
In new lands as they unfold.

Other Worlds Have I

I grew up in a mountain
Canyon next to a tidal river
And fields that grew from sandstone
That had been set and seasoned.
Home felt like fine ocean sand.
My emotions sometimes moved in sync
With the tides. On cloudless nights,
I watched the Moon and images
Far above me and I absorbed
The words my mother would say
As she looked to the heavens:
"Other worlds have I." She believed
The church of her childhood taught
That idea. Though, we couldn't find
It in the Bible or other books
That they shared. Incredible revelations
Such as this were not unique.
She told of aliens and ghosts.
As a child of the church,
She would attend the early services
With her grandparents, who lived in
A home with a flat roof.
One weekend, they went home early.
When they pulled up, she saw
A saucer-shaped ship (with three legs)
Populated with aliens she could witness
Moving past the windows. She whispered
With fear and surprise to her

Grandparents. They said that they saw
Nothing. She told me this story
Whenever I asked. She said it
Was the truth. She was not
Sure why they could not see
What was so clearly above them.
She once saw an unsettled apparition
In the old, rundown ranch house
She and my father moved into
And achingly remodeled after they married.
The ghost sometimes slammed a bedroom's
Door until she one day yelled,
"This is my home now. Leave!
We are staying. You must go."
That night, upon waking, she heard
A sound downstairs. As she stood
At the top of the stairs—
Below—she saw an old man
Dressed in a white suit staring
Observantly. The ghost was silent. Light
Flickered and he was gone. After
That night, doors did not slam,
And he was not seen again.
I don't know what is true.
I only know some people see scenes
Others call dreams while the Moon sails
Through the sky while my steady hands
Follow Earth's old branches to new streams.

Flower Arrangements

I always love the arranged flowers
In the rooms. The arrangements shower
Our home with warmth and abundance.
I often carry their beauty to
Ugly places where pain colors sound.
I marvel that anyone can care
Enough about sharing the little things
In life—the extra energy required
In the garden to grow flowers,
Ferns, and other flora for vases
In the spaces that appear central
To a joyful and colorful existence.
Fragrant mornings lead to meaningful moments
Memorialized in my mission to help
You see how much you mean
To me and all who know
You. Know, when I arrange flowers,
Your love of beauty is sown.

Cutting Boards

In my youth, the Oregon Coast
Wasn't merely the majestic, soundly sea.
Most lived near bays and rivers.
Everyone had a favorite fragrant tree
Species. Lumber flowed from sturdy saw
Mills, and massive wood chip piles
Were as tall as old-growth timber.
Hills of money, memorably ocean bound
As wood chips, were valued to
Paper ideas in an unwrapped world.
Ink's mate journeyed over the ocean's
And far land's rough, winding paths.
Myrtlewood was in every kitchen. Cutting
Boards were a metaphor for harvests
Made deep in the damp forests.
Corporate capital and careful cutters fought
Both each other and private elements.
The timber in the tracks deeply
Held their hopeful and shared imagination.
Many believed in an inexhaustible harvest.
Size and scale were often confused
For constant renewal. Now—cutting boards,
Framed with wood from the forests,
Hold hands with ancestors who remain.

Retired Neighbors

Someday, I hope you are lucky
Enough to live near retired neighbors
Whose words reveal sound, deep roots
And whose actions are trails along
Partitions that provide space for each
Day to be a dahlia. May
Your retired neighbors' waves reach you
Gently like soft breezes around corners.
May unhurried occasions on your path
Earn you unannounced home visits expected.
May you (like them) tend to
The harvests of invitation as life
Lightly sips the tea of tales
From the ones who are slowly
Becoming the best able to teach
How important it is to enjoy
The golden leaves of leisurely days.

Afterword

Poems from the collection *Coos River Reverberations: Poems of River, Farm & Forest* (2021) had adjustments made to stanzas. The poems selected for this collection are now mostly quatrains and quintains. In most cases, the poems are the same as before. In the case of *Looking Out the Classroom Window*, I removed two stanzas to improve clarity. In all cases, I worked hard to stay true to the essence of the original poems.

The fourteen poems from *Amble: Poems (2021)* were extensively revised from the original collection and became (loose) prose sonnets. I was inspired by Diane Seuss's Pulitzer Prize for Poetry book: *frank: sonnets*. Two of my collections of poetry: *Idling Intuitions: Poems* and *Mast Years: Poems* use a similar prose format called isoverbal prosody or "word count." Instead of a limit to the number of lines in the poem, line length is set to create a "loose metrical system." Word count is a technique discussed by Lewis Turco in *The New Book of Forms: A Handbook of Poetics*.

Thank you, Michael McGriff, for the many book recommendations over the last few years as well as the idea to create this new and selected poetry collection. I would also like to thank my lovely wife, Sarah, for her steadfast support and encouragement of my writing. This book also goes out to everyone who has read or helped edit my first book, *Coos River Reverberations: Poems of River, Farm & Forest*. I hope this new book finds you well and that you enjoy what you find here.

GUY CRAIG is from Coos Bay, Oregon, where he grew up along the South Fork Coos River. He lives in Tigard, Oregon, and spends most of his free time in the Coos River Valley. He holds a Master of Science in Special Education from the University of Oregon and a Bachelor of Science in Psychology from Portland State University. He was a high school special education teacher and college academic advisor. Guy is the author of five poetry collections: *Coos River Reverberations: Poems of River, Farm & Forest (2021); Amble: Poems (2021) Idling Intuitions: Poems (2022); Mast Years: Poems (2022); Only You Can Say: New and Selected Poems (2025).*

www.ingramcontent.com/pod-product-compliance
Lightning Source LLC
Chambersburg PA
CBHW042320090526
44585CB00024BA/2710